The Hidden Contracts: How Governments Enslave the People

Roger Davies

Published by TWON Publications, 2025.

THE HIDDEN CONTRACTS: HOW GOVERNMENTS ENSLAVE THE PEOPLE

First edition. September 17, 2025.

ISBN: 979-8232411718

Written by Roger Davies.

Table of Contents

This book is dedicated to all who stand in honour when it is costly, who speak truth when it is unfashionable, and who guard their neighbours when policy turns cruel.

"The chains are not on your wrists. They are on your mind — and they fall away the moment you say no."

Introduction

Freedom is the birthright of every man and woman. It does not come from government, it does not depend on a constitution, and it is not granted by an authority figure wearing robes or crowns.

Freedom is given by the Creator, and it is inseparable from life itself.

Yet despite this truth, most of humanity lives in a condition of bondage. The tragedy is that few realise it. The chains are not physical. They are made of paper, signatures, registrations, licences, and agreements.

They are contracts no one knowingly signed, yet everyone is told to obey.

This book is about those hidden contracts. It will show you how governments, all their parliaments, courts, councils and agencies, build their power not through brute force but through deception.

They trick the living man or woman into standing as a legal fiction, a corporation, a Strawman.

They offer benefits and privileges that seem harmless, but in truth are traps that bind you into servitude. Once you understand how the system works, you can begin to step out of it.

You can reclaim your standing as a free man or woman.

The journey begins at birth. From the moment a baby enters the world, paperwork is prepared. The birth is registered, a certificate is issued, and a legal entity is created.

That entity looks like you, sounds like you, and bears your name in capital letters.

It is not you. It is a corporate construct, owned and controlled by the state. This is the first hidden contract, the one that allows all others to follow.

With the creation of the Strawman, governments build an artificial person that can be taxed, licensed, fined, and regulated.

Most people never question this. They go to school, where they are taught obedience to authority and blind faith in officialdom. They are told that government is the source of order and law.

They are taught to memorise rules, to sit in silence, to ask permission for every action.

From childhood, the conditioning begins. By the time adulthood comes, the individual has accepted slavery as normal. They believe they are free while living under constant control.

Consider the world you live in. You need permission to drive a car, to build on your own land, to marry, even to fish. Each of these permissions comes in the form of a licence. And what is a licence?

It is a piece of paper that says you may do what was already lawful so long as you pay tribute and obey conditions.

The need for a licence is proof that freedom has been replaced with servitude. When you ask for permission, you admit you are not sovereign. You admit you are property.

Taxation follows the same pattern. No law compels the living man to pay income tax, council tax, or VAT. Yet people pay, year after year, because they are told it is compulsory. In truth, tax is a matter of contract.

You are invited to declare yourself a taxpayer by signing forms, registering accounts, and complying with notices.

Once you have consented, the system enforces payment as if it were law. But without consent, there is no obligation. This is the hidden trick.

What looks like law is in fact commercial obligation disguised as statute.

Courts reveal the deception most clearly. Walk into a courtroom and you will see the trappings of authority, gowns, wigs, symbols, flags. But look closer. The judge is not there to apply law, but to enforce contracts.

The courtroom operates under Admiralty jurisdiction, the law of the sea, where everything is commerce and everything is property.

This is why your name appears in capital letters, why you are asked to "stand" and "plead," why silence is taken as consent. You are treated as a vessel, a corporate entity, not a living soul.

Police officers, too, act not as guardians of peace but as agents of enforcement. Their uniforms, badges, and warrant cards are corporate insignia. Their true role is to ensure compliance with contracts.

When they stop you on the road or knock on your door, they are not enforcing natural law.

They are attempting to create joinder, to trick you into standing as the Strawman. The moment you identify yourself by name, the moment you agree to their questions, you step into the contract. Knowledge is the only defence.

Education and media play their part in maintaining the illusion. Schools teach obedience. Television and newspapers ridicule anyone who challenges government authority. Those who speak of sovereignty are dismissed as conspiracy theorists.

The masses are encouraged to laugh at the very idea of freedom.

This is how control is preserved, not by reason, not by evidence, but by ridicule and repetition. The population polices itself by mocking truth-tellers.

Debt and banking form another chain. The banks create money out of thin air, using only your signature. Loans, mortgages, and credit cards are presented as obligations, but in reality you are funding them with your own energy.

The courts then step in to enforce repayment, ensuring that the illusion of debt keeps you working for a lifetime.

Generations are trapped by this cycle, never realising that the money they repay never existed in the first place.

At every stage, the pattern is the same. The government does not force you. It invites you. It offers a contract. It relies on your consent, whether explicit or silent.

Once you have consented, it acts as though you are bound forever.

This is the essence of hidden slavery. It is voluntary servitude, created by deception, maintained by ignorance, and enforced by fear.

The purpose of this book is to expose that slavery. Each chapter will reveal one of the hidden contracts: the birth certificate, citizenship, licences, taxation, courts, police powers, education, media, debt, and banking.

It will show you not only how the system works, but also how to stand outside it.

It will arm you with maxims of law, with knowledge of your true status, with examples of others who have reclaimed their sovereignty. It will not give you freedom, that is already yours.

It will remind you of what you already are.

Ask yourself some questions as you begin this journey. Did you ever knowingly sign a contract giving government authority over you? Did you ever agree to become property of the state?

Did you ever consent to being treated as a corporation, a Strawman?

If the answer is no, then why do you act as though you are bound? The truth is simple: no one ever asked your consent. They presumed it. And unless you rebut that presumption, the system continues unchallenged.

This introduction is only the beginning. The chapters ahead will take you deeper into each aspect of the system, showing you the mechanics of control and the methods of remedy. Read them carefully. Consider them seriously.

Share them with others who are beginning to question the lies.

Freedom spreads not by force, but by knowledge. Once one person sees the hidden contracts, the spell is broken. Once enough people see, the entire system collapses.

You are a living man or woman. You are flesh and blood, not paper and ink. You are spirit, not a corporate entity. You are sovereign, not subject. The system only works if you forget this.

Remember who you are, and the chains fall away.

The journey out of slavery begins now.

Chapter 1: The Birth of the Strawman

The first hidden contract arrives with the birth certificate. A child enters the world and paperwork follows at once. Parents hear that registration is compulsory and harmless. They hear that it secures identity and services.

Few pause to ask why a living child needs a certificate to exist.

This book presents a different truth.

The birth certificate records a fact, but it does not represent the living child it names.

This corporate person is the Strawman. It is a construct that suits a commercial system. Governments and agencies operate in commerce. Commerce deals with entities that are named and recorded. The living man or woman stands outside that framework.

So, a duplicate is built on paper.

The birth certificate becomes the founding document. From that moment forward, most government letters and demands target the Strawman. The living person feels the pressure and steps into that role without realising it. The switch is subtle. The effect lasts for life.

Look at the symbols that surround official letters. Names in capital letters. Codes and numbers. References to accounts. None of this speaks to a living soul. It speaks to a corporate entry on a registry. Ships are recorded in capitals.

Companies are recorded in capitals.

Trusts are recorded in capitals. When you receive a letter that shows your name in that style, the system addresses the Strawman. The trick works because most people never learned to spot it. They respond in good faith. Their response forms joinder.

Joinder links the living person to the paper entity.

For most of human history births were recorded in family Bibles, parish books, or by the memory of kin. Life moved on without a central registry. Communities knew who was who. Bonds of duty and care arose through custom and honour.

The modern state replaced that with a registry that looks neutral but shifts power.

With registration, authority moves from family to office. People learn to believe that a child exists only once entered in that system. That belief has weight. It gives officials a foothold in family life.

It also prepares the ground for later claims over the person.

The timing matters. Parents meet this system when they are tired and emotional. A form appears. The tone is firm. The message speaks of duty and benefit. Few parents are in a mood to study terms or meanings. They sign.

No one tells them they are creating a legal person separate from the child.

No one explains the lasting effect of this act. Silence hangs over the real function of the certificate. The signature stands. The registry gains a new entry, which years later becomes the reference point for taxes, fines, and licences.

Researchers point to a link between certificates and finance. They say the entry supports bonds and credit. They say it joins the person to national obligations.

Whether you accept each financial claim or not, the pattern is clear. A paper identity is formed and then used as a handle. Through that handle the system moves money and claims rights. The living person carries the burden.

The source of the burden is a paper trail that began with the certificate.

Once you see the pattern, old letters and forms take on a new meaning.

Think about routine life events. To get a passport you are told to present the birth certificate. To open a bank account you present the birth certificate. To enrol a child in school you present the birth certificate.

The pattern repeats again and again. Each step asks you to prove the existence of the registry entry. The living person needs no proof. The living person breathes and thinks and feels. The registry entry does none of these things.

It sits in a database.

Yet every important service is tied to that entry. The system trains people to live through the Strawman.

Courts reveal the structure with stark clarity. The court clerk calls a name in capitals. The judge wants you to stand and answer for that name. The room works on procedure, not truth. Standing and answering binds you to the role.

You agree to be the entity on the charge sheet.

That is joinder again. The judge proceeds as if the matter is settled. The robe, the crest, and the ritual hide a commercial process. The dispute becomes a ledger. The court concerns itself with balancing claims in a commercial forum.

The living man or woman is reduced to a debtor on paper.

Many point to signs of maritime law in these rooms. The flags and the forms. The language of appearance and consent. Whether a reader accepts the maritime link or not, the methods are clear. The tribunal seeks a voluntary appearance.

It seeks agreement.

It seeks a plea. It seeks a signature. Every step is a doorway. Every doorway invites the living person to act as the Strawman. Once that happens, the rest follows on rails. The court applies rules that fit a corporate world.

Flesh and blood fades behind the mask of the legal person.

Police officers serve as field agents for this structure. Their uniform carries badges of office. Their notebooks and devices record names and dates of birth. They ask for identity. They seek a verbal link to the registry.

A roadside stop often unfolds as an attempt to create joinder.

The words seem simple. Name. Address. Date of birth. Those answers tie the living person to the entry. Once that link is recorded, the paperwork flows. The invitation hardens into a demand.

It all rests on the first step, which is the acknowledgment of the paper name.

Education prepares people to accept this flow. Children line up and ask permission for simple acts. They learn to address authority with titles. They learn that rules outrank judgment. They learn to trust printed words over lived truth.

By the time they reach adulthood, the habit of compliance runs deep.

When an official tone speaks, they obey. When a form appears, they sign. When a summons arrives, they appear. Few stop to ask where the duty began. Few return to the original paper and question the meaning of the birth entry.

The media supports this habit. It mocks those who question registration and legal fiction. It paints them as cranks. It promotes the idea that paperwork equals civilisation. It tells the audience that freedom exists inside the lines on a form.

People absorb this story without real thought.

Fear of ridicule keeps many silent. Pride keeps others loyal to a system that harms them. The result is a culture that serves the registry first and truth second.

The heart of the problem is consent. Consent makes law. Consent binds. Consent supplies jurisdiction. The system rarely seeks informed consent. It seeks compliance. It relies on silence. It relies on habit. It relies on the power of official style.

Parents sign the first form with no informed briefing.

Later, the grown child repeats the pattern with fresh forms. A trail of signatures grows. At each step the paper person gains more weight. The living person shrinks behind the signatures and the codes.

People sometimes push back and report success. A clerk drops a case when jurisdiction is challenged early and cleanly. A demand letter is withdrawn after a robust reply. A hearing ends when no verified contract is shown.

These stories are rare in the press.

They are common in private circles. They show that consent is the key lever. They also show that the system prefers quick wins. When the living person refuses to adopt the paper role, the machine loses speed and often stops.

The goal of this chapter is not to give you a script. The goal is to open your eyes to structure. The first contract builds a framework that supports every later claim. Once you see that, every document looks different.

You start to ask plain questions.

Who is addressed. Is it the living person or the entry. Where is the agreement. Where is the duty born. Where is the signature that binds a living soul to a corporate scheme. These questions do work by themselves.

They bring clarity and peace in tense moments.

Language matters. Officials speak of persons, residents, drivers, taxpayers, debtors, and defendants. Each word points to a role that exists on paper. A living man or woman has a name, but stands above roles.

The system prefers roles because roles fit into ledgers.

Roles have numbers. Roles have fields on a screen. When you accept a role without thought, you step down from your living status. You agree to be processed. You give weight to the first contract that birthed the role.

The cure starts with careful speech.

History offers clues. The rise of central banking marched with the spread of registration. Large states sought full records of births, deaths, and property. The promise was safety and planning. The reality was control.

A ledger that counts every soul also attaches every soul to a fiscal plan.

The birth certificate feeds the census.

The census feeds taxation. Taxation feeds debt. Debt feeds control of policy.

Step back and the picture is stark. A single act in a registry room echoes through the decades.

Families sometimes try to refuse registration. They face threats and fear. They face stories about lost rights and medical care. They face friction when travelling or studying. This pressure proves the point.

If the certificate were a harmless note, refusal would not trouble the state.

The heat around refusal shows that the paper entry is a pillar. The system defends pillars. It must do so to preserve its reach.

Even those who secure an exception often find that later offices try to rebuild the entry by other means.

Ask yourself simple questions. When did you agree to be property of a corporate state. When did you authorise an agency to speak for you by default. When did you accept a role as debtor by birth.

No honest person will find a clear moment.

There is no meeting of minds and no full briefing. There is only a trail that starts in a registry and grows through life. The cure is to withdraw blind consent and stand as the living person in truth and honour.

That stand is quiet and firm.

It begins within the mind and the tongue.

Maxims of law help to frame this stand. He who fails to deny agrees. A matter must be proved by the party who asserts it. No one is obliged to accept a benefit. These short lines hold deep wisdom.

They protect the free when used with care.

They remove fear. They remind you that power rests on consent and proof.

A birth certificate proves paper facts. It does not prove that a living soul agreed to serve a corporate plan.

That missing piece is the gap through which freedom returns.

Some readers will want a list of steps. That is not the point of this book. The point is to restore sight. The moment you see the pattern, your choices change. You pause before you sign.

You read what you are asked to accept.

You refuse roles that do not honour your status. You stay peaceful. You speak with restraint. You hold to truth.

Bureaucracy feeds on fear and haste. It starves when faced with steady men and women who know who they are.

Let us return to the child in the registry room. The mother holds the baby. The father reads a form. An official watches a clock. The family stands at a fork.

One path keeps honour within the family and records the birth in private ways.

The other path feeds the registry and grows a Strawman. Most people take the second path because no one explained the choice. This book explains the choice. It shows how the first decision shapes a life in quiet but serious ways.

A story will help to make this real. A man in his thirties faced a demand from a council office. He wrote back and asked who they were addressing.

He asked whether the demand was for the entry in the registry or for the living man.

He asked for a verified contract that linked the living man to the account number on the letter.

The office sent a form reply. He asked again with patience.

Weeks passed and the matter fell silent. Nothing dramatic. No fireworks. Silence. The frame could not bear scrutiny.

Another story concerns a mother who faced a school threat over forms. She replied with calm questions. Was attendance tied to a commercial entry. Was a grant or fee due from a central fund that rested on the birth record.

What duty was owed by a living child beyond peace and honour.

The school backed down. The child learned at home for a time. Later a private arrangement was reached that respected the family. The important point is the method. Calm questions. No anger. No insults. A refusal to move unless clarity was offered.

These stories show a quiet path. They do not invite conflict. They invite clarity. They open space for the living person to stand apart from the paper role. Once that space exists, many threats lose force. A court prefers fast labels.

A clerk prefers fast ticks.

A police officer prefers fast admissions. Slow the process with honour. Ask who is addressed. Ask for the agreement. Ask for the verified duty. You will find that many storms pass when faced with light.

The first contract is the root. The chapters that follow will track the branches. Licences grow from the root. Taxes grow from the root. Debt grows from the root. Court claims grow from the root. Each branch needs the Strawman.

Each branch fails when the living person refuses to merge with the paper entry.

Study these links as you read. See the structure once and you will never forget it.

Hold to a few final points. A certificate records a fact but does not create a soul. A registry issues numbers but does not own life. An office writes rules but does not outrank truth.

A living man or woman stands above paper.

Speak that truth without anger. Live that truth with care. Teach that truth to your children. Let written roles serve you, not rule you. When you move through life with this frame, fear loses ground and freedom grows.

The chapter closes where it began. A child is born. A paper entry appears. Two paths run forward. One path leads to decades of reflex compliance. The other path leads to thoughtful consent and firm boundaries. Choose the second path.

Choose it for yourself today, even if your parents walked the other way.

The past holds no chain that knowledge cannot break. You are living. You are free by birth. Hold that line in your heart and on your tongue, and the paper world will begin to reflect it.

Chapter 2: Contracts Hidden in Plain Sight

Citizenship is presented as a badge of pride. People are told it grants rights, protections, and identity. In truth, citizenship is a form of servitude. It is a contract that binds a living man or woman to a corporate state.

Once bound, duties and obligations replace freedom.

The word citizen hides the role of subject. It makes voluntary servitude sound noble. Yet the effect is the same as chains.

The moment you accept citizenship, you place yourself under statutes, regulations, and endless demands. You agree to pay taxes. You agree to accept benefits that come with conditions. You agree to submit to laws made without your consent.

The state tells you that this is your duty.

Duty cannot exist without agreement. Citizenship is the means by which the state tricks you into agreement.

Consider how citizenship is acquired. At birth, the registry entry provides a path for the state to treat the child as a citizen. Later, the individual applies for documents like passports, driving licences, and national insurance numbers.

Each application asks for proof of citizenship.

Each application strengthens the contract. The living person is coaxed to act through the Strawman. The Strawman stands as a citizen of the corporate state. The living person stands free. Few ever realise the difference.

The passport is one of the strongest tools of this system. People believe it proves nationality and secures freedom of travel.

Yet the passport belongs to the issuing authority. Read the fine print. It is state property.

It can be revoked at will.

The holder is not the owner. The holder is a user of state property. Travel is not a right but a licensed privilege. This is the essence of citizenship as servitude. You are told that the passport liberates you.

In truth it binds you to terms you did not negotiate.

National insurance numbers serve a similar purpose. Without them, no formal employment is possible. Yet obtaining one ties you to the tax system. You are told it funds your retirement or health care.

In reality it functions as an account number in a fiscal scheme.

Each contribution confirms your role as a taxpayer. The living man owes nothing by nature. Only the citizen role carries a duty to pay. By asking for the number, you step into that role.

You declare yourself a servant of the state's financial plan.

Consider marriage licences. Marriage is a natural union between man and woman. It needs no state involvement. Yet governments insert themselves by demanding a licence. The licence brings the union into state jurisdiction. The couple becomes a legal partnership subject to regulation.

Property division, custody, and divorce all flow from this interference.

The couple believe they are exercising a right. In truth they have begged permission.

Once more, the state defines the terms. The natural union has been converted into a contract of servitude.

Education reinforces these contracts. Children are taught to pledge loyalty to flags and institutions. They are told that citizenship is the highest honour. They are given certificates of achievement that tie their identity to the state.

The narrative is drilled in until they never question it.

By the time they reach adulthood, they identify not as free men or women but as loyal citizens. This is mental conditioning that ensures servitude will continue generation after generation.

Citizenship also acts as the basis for taxation. Governments claim that taxes are the duty of citizens. They claim benefits cannot exist without contributions. Yet look closely at the wording of tax demands. They always address the name in capitals.

They always presume citizenship.

If you are not a citizen, the demand has no lawful basis. Citizenship is the hook on which taxation hangs. The living man or woman does not owe tribute to a corporate entity. Only the paper role of citizen does.

The media glorifies citizenship. People are shown ceremonies where immigrants take oaths. They are told these oaths create unity and opportunity. They are never told that these oaths bind the individual into lifelong duties.

They are never told that the oath is a contract that removes natural freedom.

The spectacle hides the truth. It sells servitude as celebration. The crowd applauds while chains are fastened.

Maxims of law state that consent makes law. Citizenship is consent. Once you declare yourself a citizen, you give consent to be governed.

You cannot complain of tyranny if you volunteer for it. The state relies on ignorance.

It knows that if people saw citizenship for what it is, many would refuse it.

That is why schools, media, and officials repeat the word citizen with pride. They repeat it until no one questions it.

History shows how citizenship has been used to strip freedom. In ancient empires, citizenship carried both privilege and heavy duty. It required tribute and military service. The Roman citizen could be taxed, conscripted, and punished by Roman law.

The empire expanded by offering citizenship as a prize.

In reality it was a chain. Modern states follow the same pattern. They speak of citizenship as inclusion. In truth it is the same trap with modern symbols.

A citizen cannot stand as sovereign. The two conditions are opposites. Sovereign means master of one's self. Citizen means servant of the state. A sovereign lives by natural law and honour. A citizen lives by statute and regulation.

A sovereign owes no tribute.

A citizen pays endlessly. A sovereign moves by right. A citizen moves by licence. The choice is clear. Yet the system never presents it as a choice. It presents citizenship as natural, automatic, and unavoidable. That is the deception.

Examples prove the point. Men and women who have declared themselves outside citizenship have challenged tax, debt, and regulation.

Some have succeeded in having cases dropped. They stood firm as living beings, not corporate citizens.

They refused to accept the title of taxpayer or resident. They demanded proof of contract. In many cases officials backed away. These stories reveal the weakness of the system. It cannot compel without consent. It thrives only when consent is presumed.

Think of the word resident. It is another trap. To call yourself a resident is to accept that you reside in a corporate district subject to rules. To call yourself a citizen is to accept that you belong to a corporate state.

Each word is a role.

Each role is a contract. The living man or woman can state simply: I am a man. I am a woman. I live, breathe, and stand under natural law. That statement places you outside the roles. That statement breaks the spell.

The remedy begins with awareness. Stop calling yourself a citizen. Stop signing forms that declare you one. Stop begging for rights that already belong to you by birth. Learn to separate the Strawman from the living being.

Let the Strawman carry roles and duties if it must.

Let the living being remain free. Speak this truth calmly but firmly. When asked if you are a citizen, pause. Ask what that word means. Ask for proof of contract. Ask who offered terms and when you agreed.

You will find that answers are vague or absent.

Some men and women have gone further. They have written notices to withdraw consent to citizenship.

They have declared their standing as living beings under common law.

These notices use maxims, affidavits, and conditional acceptance. They are ignored at first.

Persistence has power.

Once an official record exists of refusal, the presumption of consent weakens. The living man or woman begins to step out of the cage.

This does not mean isolation. It does not mean living without community. It means forming bonds on equal terms. It means private agreements between men and women of honour. It means trade and cooperation without state interference.

It means standing in freedom rather than servitude.

The state wants people to fear this path. It wants them to believe chaos will follow. In truth, honour brings order. Communities that stand outside the state prove it every day.

You must ask yourself hard questions. Do you serve because you fear punishment? Do you obey because you were told you are a citizen? Do you accept burdens that are not yours because you fear ridicule?

These are the chains that bind most people.

They are mental more than physical. Once the mind sees through them, the chains fall away. Fear is the only real weapon the state has. Knowledge breaks fear.

Let us close this chapter with a clear statement. Citizenship is not freedom. It is servitude dressed in fine words. It is the mechanism by which the state gains power over the living. It is the reason taxes, licences, and debts attach.

It is the mask that hides slavery.

To reclaim your birthright, you must lay it aside. You must stand not as a citizen but as a living man or woman. That stand is simple.

It requires no paperwork, no licence, no oath. It requires only truth.

The chapters ahead will build on this knowledge. They will show how every demand rests on roles like citizen, taxpayer, and resident. They will show how to refuse those roles with honour.

They will show the victories of those who have stood firm.

Once you see the pattern, it cannot be unseen. The word citizen will never sound the same again. You will hear the chain hidden inside it. And you will know that you were never born to wear it.

Freedom is not tied to citizenship. It is not created by statute. It flows from life itself. When you remember this truth, the word citizen loses its hold. You no longer fear the loss of benefits or papers.

You see them as traps, not treasures.

This shift is the first act of freedom. It is the point where servitude ends and sovereignty begins.

Chapter 3: Licences: Permission as Ownership

Licences are one of the clearest signs of hidden slavery. A licence is described as permission from the state to do something that would otherwise be unlawful. Driving, marrying, building, hunting, trading, or fishing are not crimes in themselves.

They are natural acts of life.

Why must a man or woman beg permission at all?

It reduces free action into a grant from the state.

A licence always comes with conditions. You must pay a fee. You must follow terms. You must submit to penalties. In other words, you agree that the state owns the right and lends it back to you.

The living man or woman owns every right by birth.

A licence reverses the truth. It says you are a subject, not sovereign. It says you hold rights only by grant. This inversion is the essence of hidden contracts. It transforms rights into privileges and freedom into servitude.

Driving licences prove the point. The roads were built by the people. Travel is a natural right. Yet the state demands you apply for permission to use your own roads. Without a licence you risk fines or arrest.

The licence itself is the trap, because applying creates a contract with the state.

When you apply, you contract. You agree to statutes that treat you as a driver, not a traveller. A driver is a role in commerce.

It is one who transports goods for hire. That is why laws regulating drivers exist.

Yet every man and woman is forced to adopt the role of driver.

Marriage licences follow the same pattern. Marriage is an ancient union that predates government. It is rooted in nature and honour. No paper is needed for man and woman to join. Yet states demand a licence.

By applying, the couple enters state jurisdiction.

Their union becomes subject to statutes. Property division, custody battles, and state oversight flow from that act. The state intrudes into the most private of unions under colour of a licence. What should be sacred becomes regulated.

Business licences extend the trap into commerce. Trade is as old as humanity. Men and women exchanged goods long before states existed. Yet today no one may trade openly without a licence. The licence carries taxes, inspections, and compliance rules.

Failure brings penalties.

The state presents this as consumer protection. In truth it is revenue generation and control. It ensures that every exchange enriches the system. It ensures that independent trade cannot flourish outside the corporate framework.

Consider hunting and fishing licences. The earth provides food for all. Rivers, forests, and seas were once open to those who lived nearby. Now access is sold back under licence. Without permission, a man feeding his family risks fines or jail.

The licence says that nature itself is owned by the state.

It says you must pay tribute to harvest food. This is slavery in its purest form. You are told you need papers to eat from your own land and water.

Building permits are another licence trap. A man cannot raise a home on his own land without permission. He must submit drawings and fees. He must wait for approval. If the state refuses, his natural right is denied.

The idea that a free man must ask for leave to shelter his family is absurd.

Yet the system enforces it daily. The result is dependence and debt. People spend lifetimes paying mortgages because they are blocked from simple building. The licence feeds the banks and binds the people.

Look closely and you will see that every licence is linked to the Strawman. Applications always ask for the registered name, date of birth, and proof of identity. They are contracts with the legal fiction, not the living being.

The living man or woman needs no licence to act within natural law.

The Strawman is the one who asks for permission. When you act as the Strawman, you accept the role of subject. You agree to be governed. The system never tells you this openly. It hides behind forms and fees.

Maxims of law tell us that silence is consent. The state relies on this. When you apply for a licence without protest, you consent. When you pay renewal fees, you consent. When you accept penalties, you consent. Consent makes law.

The state has no lawful authority over the living.

It has only contracts. Licences are the most common form of those contracts. They are voluntary servitude presented as duty.

History shows how licences expanded. In early times, licences were rare. They covered narrow fields like taverns or markets.

Over time states expanded them into every area of life. Each new licence created a new stream of revenue.

Each new licence deepened control.

Today most people cannot imagine life without them. They accept that marriage, driving, trading, or building require approval. They never ask when or why natural rights became privileges.

They never ask who granted the state the power to sell rights back to them.

Examples prove the point. Men and women who have refused licences have sometimes succeeded. A man who drove without a licence challenged a court to show a contract. The case collapsed when no contract was produced.

A couple married without a licence in private ceremony and lived by their vows without state interference.

A family built a home quietly without permits and later proved lawful ownership. These stories show that the system fears exposure. It backs down when its lack of true authority is revealed.

The media ridicules such stories. It paints those who reject licences as lawbreakers. It warns of danger and chaos. It never admits that licences are tools of profit and control. The ridicule is designed to keep people obedient.

Fear of being mocked or punished keeps most people in line.

Yet history honours those who stood firm. The pioneers, settlers, and builders of the past lived without licences. They thrived by courage and honour. The same spirit lives today in those who reject hidden contracts.

The remedy begins with knowledge. You must see that a licence is not proof of safety or honour.

It is a contract of servitude. You must choose whether to act as the Strawman or as the living man.

If you apply, you consent.

If you decline, you remain free. The choice is yours. Freedom requires courage. Servitude requires nothing but habit. Each time you are asked for a licence, pause. Ask what crime exists without it. Ask who was harmed. Ask what contract you signed.

The answers reveal the truth.

Practical steps follow. When faced with licence demands, respond with conditional acceptance. Agree only if proof is shown that a duty exists. Ask for the contract. Ask for the verified obligation. If none appears, stand as the living being.

Do not argue or fight.

Simply withdraw consent. This approach has saved many from fines and penalties. It shifts the burden back to the system. It forces officials to admit they rely only on assumption. Assumption has no lawful power without consent.

Citizenship and licences are linked. Citizenship creates the role. Licences enforce it. Together they form a cage. The man or woman who sees this cage can step out of it. They can live by natural law, not statute.

They can trade, travel, marry, build, and live with honour.

They can choose freedom. The state cannot stop this without consent. It can only scare and ridicule. Its power is illusion. Once seen, the illusion breaks.

Ask yourself simple questions. Did you need a licence to breathe. Did you need one to speak. Did you need one to love.

Then why should you need one to travel, to marry, to trade, or to build. The answer is simple.

You do not.

You were free at birth. Every licence you accept is a step into slavery. Every licence you refuse is a step into freedom.

Licences are the clearest expression of hidden contracts. They take natural rights and turn them into privileges. They are sold back at a price. They keep men and women in fear of losing permission. They turn free souls into subjects.

To break this cycle you must see it.

Once you see it, you cannot unsee it. The licence becomes what it is: proof of slavery. Reject it, and you stand free.

Consider the psychological hold licences create. From a young age people are told that without permission they are reckless or criminal. This implants fear. Fear ensures compliance more than force ever could.

The threat of losing a licence keeps many obedient even when no harm was done.

This proves the licence is not about safety. It is about obedience.

Licences also generate vast revenue streams. Renewal fees, penalty charges, inspections, and mandatory courses all feed the treasury. These funds support the very system that limits freedom. The citizen pays to be bound. The sovereign would never agree to such a bargain.

Another angle is dependency. By tying health care, pensions, or access to services to licensed activity, the state deepens control. A man fears losing his driving licence because it may cost him his job.

A trader fears losing a business licence because it ends his livelihood.

Dependency secures compliance where brute law could not.

Finally, reflect on the deeper message of licences. They declare that the state owns what nature and God provided. They say travel, marriage, trade, food, and shelter are property of the state. This lie stands only if people consent.

Withdraw consent, and the truth shines clear: the living man and woman were free before the first licence was ever written.

The chapters ahead will build on this knowledge. They will show how taxation, courts, and police use licences to enforce servitude. They will show remedies that free men and women have used.

They will prepare you to stand outside the system with peace and honour.

This journey is not easy. It requires courage. But courage is the mark of the sovereign. The time has come to live as you were born: free.

Chapter 4: Taxation, The Harvest of the Strawman

Taxation is sold as the foundation of society. Politicians say it funds services, builds schools, and protects the weak. The slogan is that tax is the price of civilisation. But civilisation comes from honour, work, and community, not from forced tribute.

Tax is not law but contract.

It is an invitation made to look like a duty. No man or woman is born owing money to a government. Tribute belongs to slavery and conquest, not to free people.

Income tax is the clearest example. Wages are docked before they ever reach the worker. Employers act as tax collectors, handing over part of a man's labour to the state. The worker never signed a contract agreeing to this theft.

The demand is addressed to a name in capitals, the Strawman, not the living soul.

The system assumes consent because the worker remains silent. Silence is then used as proof of agreement. In truth no agreement was ever made.

Council tax operates the same way. Councils print demands that look like court orders. They rely on fear. Yet no wet ink signature of a judge appears. No signed contract exists. The summonses are produced by councils themselves, not by courts.

When challenged, many councils back down or quietly withdraw cases.

The reason is simple. They cannot prove a binding contract with the living man or woman.

Value added tax illustrates the trick in commerce.

Shops and businesses add it to every bill. Customers pay without question.

But what is actually happening? The state assumes that every transaction is commercial activity between corporate entities.

The moment your Strawman is invoked, the tax attaches.

The living man exchanging his labour or produce is outside this commercial net unless he consents. Consent is the hidden key again.

National Insurance shows the same pattern. People are told it is for pensions and health. But the money vanishes into government accounts. The National Insurance number is just another account number for the Strawman. Each payment confirms the role of taxpayer.

Without realising it, the living man is tricked into paying tribute for benefits he may never see.

Again, the link is consent given through application and compliance.

History shows what taxation really is. In ancient times rulers took tribute openly. Armies marched to collect it. Conquerors looted gold and grain. The modern state discovered that deception works better than force.

By convincing people that tax is their duty, rulers make slaves work willingly.

They are proud to pay. They believe they are helping society. In truth they are maintaining their own chains.

Look at the paperwork. A tax return begins with a declaration: I am a taxpayer. The form asks you to confirm the role and sign. Once you do, you have made the contract for them.

Council tax demands ask you to confirm occupancy.

Business tax forms ask you to apply for numbers. Every piece of paper is an offer.

By signing or paying, you accept. The system never forces. It only tricks you into volunteering.

Courts reveal the fraud. Tax hearings take place in administrative courts, not true courts of record. Clerks rubber stamp judgments. Judges act as bankers balancing accounts. When you appear and answer as the Strawman, you create jurisdiction.

If you challenge jurisdiction and demand proof of contract, cases often collapse.

That is why most tax cases are settled out of sight. The system does not want the fraud examined under oath.

Employers are a vital link in the chain. They deduct tax through PAYE as if it were compulsory. Yet no contract exists where the worker authorised them to take his wages. Employers act as unpaid tax agents under threat of penalties.

They pass the burden onto workers without question.

This is another example of hidden contracts where fear and assumption replace proof and consent.

The media keeps people compliant. Newspapers shame those who resist tax. Television warns of prison. Journalists never ask for proof of obligation. They repeat the slogan that tax funds hospitals and schools.

The lie is never challenged because fear is more useful than truth.

Those who question it are mocked as extremists. Ridicule becomes a weapon as sharp as any fine.

Schools teach the same story. Children learn that good citizens pay tax. They are told it is noble and fair.

They are never taught about contracts, consent, or the difference between the Strawman and the living being.

By the time they leave school, obedience is ingrained.

The habit of paying tribute is planted before they earn their first coin.

Examples exist of men and women standing against tax. Some reply to demands with conditional acceptance, asking for proof of a lawful obligation. Some challenge council summonses and see them dropped.

Others refuse to act as taxpayers and watch as cases fade away when no contract can be produced.

These victories are not publicised. They are kept quiet to protect the illusion.

Debt and tax are twin chains. Both rely on the same trick. A demand is issued to the Strawman. The living man consents by silence or by signing. Courts enforce the paper, not the truth.

When the demand is questioned, the fraud is exposed.

This is why banks and tax offices prefer intimidation to open proof. They know they cannot prove what does not exist.

Maxims of law strip away the deception. Consent makes law. He who fails to deny agrees. The burden of proof lies on he who asserts. Apply these maxims to taxation and the fraud collapses.

The state cannot prove consent of the living man.

It can only wave papers that show assumptions. Without consent there is no contract. Without contract there is no tax.

Practical remedy begins with awareness. When a tax letter arrives, read it as an offer.

Ask yourself who is being addressed. Ask where the contract was signed. Ask when you agreed to be a taxpayer.

If no answer is given, stand in honour and decline the offer.

Reply with conditional acceptance: you will pay if proof of obligation is provided. No proof will come. The offer falls away when light is shone on it.

This is not refusal. It is clarity. You are not avoiding duty. You are exposing fraud. You are saying: show me the contract. Without it, I owe nothing. This calm approach removes fear. It returns power to the living being.

It reminds officials that assumption is not law.

It teaches them that silence is not agreement when truth is spoken.

The deeper lesson is that taxation is a chain only because people believe it is. The belief is stronger than iron. Once the belief breaks, the chain breaks too. No army enforces income tax on every man and woman.

No judge can conjure a contract out of silence once it is challenged.

The fraud continues only because people accept it without thought.

Ask yourself now. Did you ever sign an agreement to pay income tax. Did you ever consent to council tax. Did you ever request VAT on your shopping. You did not. You were told it was law.

Being told is not the same as consent.

Agreement requires consent. Consent requires knowledge. You never gave it.

Taxation is tribute of the slave. It is hidden beneath words of duty and law.

But once you see it, the mask falls. The living man owes nothing to a corporate fiction. You were born free.

You remain free unless you consent to chains.

The invitation to pay tribute arrives in the post each year. You can accept or decline. The choice is yours.

The next chapters will show how courts, police, and banks all use the same method. They rely on hidden contracts, on silence, and on ignorance. Once you learn to see the trick, it loses power. Taxation is one of the greatest lies.

Break it, and the whole system begins to crumble.

The language of tax demands reveals much. Phrases like ‘you must’ and ‘it is required by law’ are used to instil fear. But if you read carefully, the documents always stop short of naming the living man or woman.

They target the role of taxpayer.

They never include a signed contract from the living being. This detail is ignored by most, yet it is the weakness that collapses the illusion when exposed.

Consider the use of threats. Penalties, surcharges, and prison are spoken of freely. These are weapons of intimidation.

They are rarely used, and when they are, it is often against those who stood in dishonour rather than those who calmly asked for proof.

The state depends on the majority being too afraid to ask questions. Fear is cheaper than force.

Another hidden layer is the use of banks. Taxes are collected through bank accounts. Payments are demanded electronically.

This creates another chain of control. Once money enters the banking system, it is no longer yours.

It is a promise of value controlled by the bank.

By tying tax to banks, the state ensures that refusing to pay is harder. Yet again, the weakness is consent. You agreed to use the bank. You agreed to link accounts. Without that, the system falters.

History offers countless examples of resistance to unfair taxation. The American colonies rebelled over taxes on tea and stamps. Farmers in medieval Europe rioted against tithes. The cry of 'no taxation without representation' shaped revolutions.

These movements were not about money but about consent.

People saw that tribute without agreement is theft. That truth has not changed.

Think also about what tax money funds. Politicians claim it pays for schools and hospitals. But vast sums go to wars, interest on debt, and projects that serve corporations. The taxpayer believes he is supporting society.

In reality he is financing his own enslavement.

He pays for the very machine that robs him.

Case studies from recent years show the cracks. In some local councils, tens of thousands of summonses are issued automatically. Many collapse when individuals challenge them. In courts, demands for signed contracts often go unanswered.

Even in tax tribunals, cases are dropped when jurisdiction is questioned.

These examples prove that the power of taxation is paper thin when tested with honour.

Practical remedy also involves knowledge of maxims.

A man who knows that 'consent makes the law' and 'no one is obliged to accept a benefit' can stand with calm. He sees the letter as an offer, not a command.

He knows the burden of proof lies on the accuser.

He uses these truths to turn fear into strength. Knowledge arms the free man more than weapons ever could.

The emotional side must also be addressed. Many fear the judgement of neighbours and peers if they question tax. They fear being called selfish or unpatriotic. But truth is not decided by popularity.

The same was said of every man and woman who resisted unjust rule.

Courage requires standing apart from the crowd. It requires loyalty to honour above fear of ridicule.

Future generations depend on the choices made now. If this generation continues to pay tribute without question, the chains will only tighten. If enough men and women stand in truth, the system will weaken. Children will learn that freedom is possible.

They will inherit courage instead of fear.

That is the true duty owed to society, not blind payment of tribute.

At its heart, taxation is a psychological contract. The paperwork is secondary. The real contract is in the mind. People believe they owe, so they pay. The remedy is mental as much as legal.

The moment you know you owe nothing, you change your posture.

You stop shaking when letters arrive. You stop fearing officials. You stand calm, and the system senses it. Fear feeds it, courage starves it.

Finally, remember that honour is the remedy. Refusing in anger leads to conflict. Refusing with calm questions leads to freedom. The man or woman who asks for proof, who stands in peace, and who refuses to lie, walks free.

The chains fall away not with violence but with truth spoken clearly.

Chapter 5: Courts, The Temples of the Strawman

Courts are presented as houses of justice. They are sold to the public as neutral places where disputes are settled and truth is upheld. Yet the deeper reality is that courts are temples of the Strawman.

They exist to transfer the living man or woman into the role of a legal fiction.

Once this transfer is made, jurisdiction is claimed, and the process unfolds as commerce disguised as law.

The first act of every court is to call a name. That name appears in capital letters, the mark of the Strawman. If you rise and answer, you have agreed to be the representative of that corporate entity.

This small action gives the judge power he did not have before.

Jurisdiction is not taken, it is given. It is given through consent in the form of appearance and response.

The architecture and ritual of courts are designed to support this illusion. The judge sits elevated like a banker above his clients. Robes and wigs create distance. Crests and flags display symbols of authority. Even the language is ritualised.

All of it communicates that you are in a place of higher power.

The purpose is psychological: to weaken the will of the man or woman before the legal trickery even begins.

Language itself is the next layer of control. Words like 'defendant', 'claimant', 'plea', 'jurisdiction', and 'order' are all terms of commerce. They do not describe living men and women but roles within a contract.

When you accept these words without challenge, you step into those roles.

Once you have taken the role, the court can treat you as property of the system. Words create contracts when they are spoken in ignorance.

The dock is another symbol that exposes the truth. The man or woman stands inside a box, fenced in as if cargo on a ship. The word 'dock' comes from admiralty, from maritime trade.

The accused is treated as goods in transit, not as a living being.

This is why so many believe courts operate under maritime law. The signs are visible in every corner of the courtroom.

Criminal trials show the deception clearly. The charge is read against the Strawman name. The accused is told to plead guilty or not guilty. Both pleas are traps. A plea is an agreement to the contract.

By entering it, you have consented to the process.

The only honest path is to challenge jurisdiction. Ask who is being addressed. Ask for the contract that binds the living man. This question unsettles the court because it exposes the trick that sustains its power.

Family courts reveal the cruelty of this system. Parents are reduced to applicants and respondents. Children are treated as wards of the state. The language of family and honour is replaced with terms of policy and statute.

Once parents accept the licence to marry, the state claims an interest in the children.

The court enforces that claim with cold efficiency. Families are torn apart not by justice but by commerce disguised as care.

Civil cases, from debt claims to council summonses, follow the same pattern. The paperwork is aimed at the Strawman. The court calls the name. The man answers. Jurisdiction is granted.

From then on, the case is processed as if it were a balance sheet.

The judge is not a seeker of truth but a manager of accounts. Victory or loss is decided by paperwork, not by natural law.

The role of lawyers confirms this reality. They are not servants of the people but officers of the court. Their duty is to the system, not the client. They speak in coded terms that exclude the ordinary man. Their language creates dependency.

They are trained to ensure that the Strawman system is maintained.

The living man who speaks for himself exposes the illusion. This is why courts discourage self-representation.

Examples exist of men and women who refused to play the role. Some have asked simple questions: Who is being addressed. Where is the contract. What proof shows that I consented. Many of these cases end quietly. Hearings are adjourned.

Cases are dropped.

Officials retreat rather than answer. These small victories prove that the court has no power over the living soul who refuses to consent.

The media keeps the illusion alive. Films and television glorify trials.

Judges are shown as wise and impartial. Lawyers are heroes. The message is repeated endlessly: the court is the place where justice lives.

In reality, the court is the place where contracts are enforced.

It is where the Strawman is bound tighter. The truth is hidden behind a screen of drama and ritual.

Schools prepare children to obey courts long before they ever enter one. They are taught that law and justice are the same. They are told to respect authority and never to question it. They are never taught about strawmen, jurisdiction, or consent.

By the time they reach adulthood, the conditioning is complete.

They walk into courts already believing they have no choice but to obey.

The symbols of submission are everywhere. Standing when the judge enters. Addressing him as 'your honour'. Waiting to be told when to speak. These are rituals of hierarchy, not of justice. By following them without thought, you consent to the illusion.

Yet these rituals have no force if you refuse them politely and firmly.

They depend on your agreement, not on truth.

Case law is filled with hints that jurisdiction is voluntary. Judgments admit that statutes require acceptance. Yet these truths are buried in language that few can read. They are not shared with the public. The system relies on secrecy.

If everyone knew that jurisdiction rests on consent, the power of courts would collapse overnight.

Prisons reveal the commercial purpose of courts. Prisoners are treated as commodities.

Each body generates revenue through contracts with corporations. This is why prison populations grow even when crime falls. The court feeds the prison system, and the prison system feeds commerce.

The living man is reduced to a number on a balance sheet once again.

Remedy begins with knowledge. The first step is to see the court as it truly is. The second step is to remain calm. Fear is the weapon of the court. It relies on men and women trembling before robes and wigs.

When you stand firm and ask simple questions, the power weakens.

Honour and truth are stronger than ritual and illusion.

Practical steps include refusing to answer to the name in capitals. Asking for the contract that binds you. Demanding proof of jurisdiction. Declining to plead unless evidence is shown. Speaking as the living man or woman, not as a role.

These steps do not guarantee victory, but they expose the fraud.

They plant doubt in the minds of officials. Doubt is poison to a system built on assumption.

Community adds strength. When men and women attend courts to observe, record, and support, the illusion is threatened. Courts thrive in secrecy. They fear exposure. A single camera or a group of witnesses can change the atmosphere.

Light breaks the spell of fear.

It reminds all present that authority exists only by consent.

The lesson of history is that courts have always served power.

From royal courts enforcing tribute to colonial courts enforcing empire, the pattern is constant. The robe and the gavel may change, but the purpose remains: to extract wealth and obedience.

This truth must be faced if freedom is to be reclaimed.

Ask yourself simple questions. Did you ever sign a contract agreeing to be bound by a judge. Did you ever consent to be a defendant. Did you ever agree to be processed as an account. The answer is always no.

The fraud rests on silence.

Break the silence, and the fraud collapses.

Courts are temples of the Strawman. They stand as pillars of the system, yet their foundation is paper and presumption. Once you see them for what they are, fear dissolves. The robe is cloth, the bench is wood, the judgment is paper.

Truth stands above them.

Honour belongs to the living man or woman, not to the corporate fiction. That is the way to freedom.

Even small details like titles carry weight. Calling a judge 'your honour' assumes he possesses honour by office alone. True honour comes from action, not from titles. By using such language, people hand respect to those who have not earned it.

40

Words shape reality, and in courts words are weapons.

Chapter 6: Police, The Enforcers of Policy

Police are presented to the people as guardians of safety. They are described as protectors of the weak and defenders of peace. The uniform, the badge, the flashing lights all create an image of service and honour.

Yet behind this image lies the true purpose of policing.

Police are not servants of the people but enforcers of policy. They do not uphold natural law. They enforce statutes, regulations, and corporate codes. Their task is not to protect freedom but to maintain control and revenue for the state.

The very name "police" gives away their function. It comes from "policy." A police officer enforces policy. Policy is not law. Policy is a set of corporate rules written by governments acting as corporations.

Natural law is simple: do no harm, cause no loss, commit no fraud.

Policy adds endless layers of statutes and regulations. When a police officer stops a man on the road, it is not because harm has been caused. It is because a policy has been breached.

The system calls this law, but in truth it is commerce.

Uniforms and badges are powerful tools of control. The uniform removes individuality and creates an aura of authority. The badge is a corporate shield, often displaying crowns, numbers, and symbols of state power. These symbols are designed to trigger compliance.

They tell the mind: obey.

The man or woman confronted by a uniform often forgets that the officer is simply an employee of a corporation. Authority is assumed, not proven. The uniform is the mask of power.

Traffic enforcement is one of the clearest examples. Roads are built by the people and for the people. Travel is a natural right. Yet police patrol roads as if they were private property. They stop travellers and demand licences, insurance, and registration.

None of these come from natural law.

They are policy requirements linked to the Strawman. When an officer writes a ticket, he is issuing an invoice to the legal fiction. Most pay without question. Few realise that they have consented to a contract that never needed to exist.

The police oath is another illusion. Officers swear to uphold the law and protect the people. But the "law" they enforce is not natural law. It is statute and code. They are trained to prioritise orders from superiors, not truth or justice.

Many are given quotas for arrests, tickets, or stop-and-search operations.

Their performance is measured not by peace preserved but by revenue generated. The oath is theatre that hides their role as policy enforcers.

History shows that police forces were never created for the people. In England, early constables and watchmen answered to local lords. In the United States, some of the first organised police forces grew out of slave patrols.

Elsewhere, police units were used to break strikes and crush protests.

From their very birth, police existed to protect property and power.

Their task was not to serve the free man or woman but to guard the interests of rulers and corporations.

The process of arrest exposes the commercial foundation. An officer makes a stop, issues warnings, and reads rights. The person is handcuffed, searched, and taken to a station. Each stage creates paperwork. Each form becomes an entry in an account.

The arrestee is logged, given a number, and processed as inventory.

This is why prisons are filled with "inmates" who are tracked by registration. The living being is reduced to data, and data is commerce.

Language betrays the truth. Officers are trained to speak of "subjects," "suspects," "residents," or "offenders." These are not descriptions of living men and women. They are roles within policy enforcement. Once a person is labelled, the process unfolds automatically.

The paperwork is completed, the fines are issued, the case moves forward.

The human element disappears. The officer is no longer dealing with a living soul but with a role in a contract.

Media is vital to the illusion. Films, television dramas, and news reports glorify police. They show officers solving crimes, saving lives, and risking everything for justice. In truth, most police work is administrative.

Officers spend their days filling forms, issuing tickets, and responding to minor disputes.

The media shows the rare heroic act and hides the daily grind of revenue collection. By doing so, it keeps the people loyal to the system.

Education prepares children for obedience. Schools invite officers to give talks, show off equipment, and portray themselves as friends of the community. Children are taught to respect and obey without question. They are not told that officers enforce policy, not law.

They are not told that officers are corporate employees.

By adulthood, obedience is ingrained. The badge triggers submission before thought even begins.

Examples prove the nature of police power. A man travelling without a licence may be stopped, fined, and even arrested, though no harm has been done.

A woman selling goods without a permit may be shut down, though her trade hurt no one.

These are not crimes under natural law. They are violations of policy. Police act as tax collectors in uniform. Their duty is to revenue, not to justice.

The use of force demonstrates this purpose clearly. Batons, tasers, pepper spray, and firearms are tools of compliance. They are not used to restore honour but to compel obedience. Violence covers the absence of lawful authority.

It hides the weakness of policy behind fear.

Force cannot create a contract. It can only intimidate. Once fear is removed, the contract fails.

Technology expands police power. Surveillance cameras, number-plate recognition, and facial recognition systems track movement. Drones observe public spaces. Databases record every interaction. These systems are justified as tools of safety. In reality, they are commercial systems tracking the Strawman.

Every scan, every entry, every record is tied to the legal fiction.

The living being is catalogued without consent.

Private corporations blur the line further. Security firms, bailiffs, and contractors often carry out the same duties as police. They collect debts, enforce evictions, and guard property. They wear different uniforms but act under the same commercial authority.

This proves that policing is not about law but about contracts.

It is business dressed up as justice.

There are officers who join believing they will serve justice. Some later discover the truth: they are revenue collectors. Whistle-blowers have spoken of quotas, ticket targets, and pressure from superiors. Their words confirm what experience already shows.

Policing is about money and compliance.

Protecting life and property is a small part, often used to justify the larger machine of control.

Remedy begins with knowledge. A man or woman who understands that officers enforce policy, not law, approaches encounters differently. Fear fades when truth is known. Questions replace obedience. Ask: Am I being detained? Am I free to go?

Ask: Who is being addressed.

Where is the contract. These simple questions shift the balance. Officers prefer easy compliance. When faced with knowledge, many back down.

Practical steps are simple. Remain calm. Do not argue. Ask for proof of obligation. State clearly that you are a living man or woman. Decline to answer as the Strawman. Refuse to sign unless evidence of contract is produced.

By standing in honour, you expose the fraud.

The officer may press harder, but his foundation is weak. He has policy, not law. Policy requires consent. Without it, he has nothing.

Community is another remedy. When men and women record encounters, observe police actions, and support each other, the illusion weakens. Officers rely on isolation and fear. Witnesses break that power. Public scrutiny exposes misconduct.

It reminds officers that they are accountable, not absolute.

A community that stands together is harder to control.

History offers countless examples of police enforcing unjust policies. Strikers beaten for demanding fair pay. Protesters arrested for speaking truth. Communities harassed under stop-and-search powers. These are not mistakes. They are natural outcomes of a system designed to serve power.

Police protect the state, not the people.

They defend contracts, not freedom.

Ask yourself direct questions. Did you ever sign a contract agreeing to be policed? Did you ever consent to strangers ordering you about. Did you ever give permission to be treated as a suspect. The answer is no.

The system survives on assumption.

Once the assumption is broken, the fraud is exposed.

Police are enforcers of policy. They are not guardians of freedom. They serve corporations and governments as employees. Their strength comes from fear and ignorance. Knowledge removes both. When you see them as revenue collectors in uniform, the spell breaks.

They are men and women doing a job, not masters of your life.

True safety comes not from police but from community. Neighbours supporting each other, families caring for their own, people living in honour: this is real protection. Police arrive after harm has occurred. Their reports and tickets do not undo loss.

The myth of police as protectors hides the truth: freedom and safety are best defended by free people themselves.

The chapters ahead will turn to prisons, banks, and debt. Each is another arm of the system. Police are the guards at the gate. They keep the people inside the cage of hidden contracts. But the gate is not locked.

It is held shut by fear and ignorance.

Knowledge opens it. Courage walks you through. Honour keeps you free.

Chapter 7: Prisons: The Warehouses of the State

Prisons are presented to the public as houses of justice. They are described as places where criminals are punished, reformed, and prepared to re-enter society. The walls, bars, and guards are said to protect the community. Yet the deeper truth is hidden.

Prisons are not temples of justice but warehouses of the state.

They are designed not for protection but for commerce. They hold bodies as inventory and use them to generate revenue. The living man or woman is reduced to a number, an account, and an entry.

The very language of prisons reveals their nature. Men and women are not called by name but by number. They are given uniforms that erase identity. They are classified, processed, and stored. This is not the language of justice.

It is the language of warehousing.

A prisoner is cargo held by the state. He is an asset, not a soul. The prison becomes a warehouse of the Strawman, not a place of honour or truth.

History shows that imprisonment was never about justice. In ancient times, punishment was swift. Restitution, banishment, or corporal penalty resolved disputes. Prisons as long-term institutions are relatively new. They grew alongside commerce and empire.

States discovered that holding men in confinement could be profitable.

Labour could be extracted. Contracts could be written. Revenue could be generated.

The prison became an engine of commerce, not a tool of justice.

Consider debtor's prisons of the past. Men who could not pay were locked away until their families settled the account. There was no question of justice. The prison was simply a warehouse for debtors. Modern prisons are no different.

They hold men and women as security for contracts.

They generate money through government funding, corporate contracts, and prison labour. The illusion of justice covers the reality of commerce.

Every step of imprisonment is commercial. The arrest produces paperwork. The court hearing creates bonds and accounts. The sentencing creates orders and contracts. The transfer to prison generates invoices. The prisoner is logged, registered, and assigned a number.

Each form is part of a chain of commerce.

The living man is turned into a commodity. He is stored like stock in a warehouse.

Symbols of the prison confirm this. Uniforms strip individuality. Numbers replace names. Cells resemble storage units. Officers count bodies daily as if checking inventory. The term "inmate" itself suggests containment within a system. This is not about justice but about management.

The prisoner is managed as property of the state, not recognised as a sovereign being.

Prison labour exposes the fraud further. Inmates are made to work for pennies or nothing at all. Their labour benefits corporations and state agencies. This is slavery by another name.

The Thirteenth Amendment in the United States openly permits forced labour as punishment for crime.

Other nations use similar policies. Men and women are turned into workers for the system, their freedom traded for contracts and profit. Warehousing bodies becomes a business model.

The economics of prisons prove the point. The more prisoners, the more funding. Private prison corporations profit from full cells. Governments allocate budgets based on numbers. Each body is worth money. This creates an incentive not for justice but for incarceration.

Police are encouraged to arrest.

Courts are encouraged to convict. The machine requires constant supply. Prisons must remain full to feed the contracts that sustain them.

Psychology is also part of the warehouse design. Confinement breaks the spirit. Stripped of freedom, a man becomes dependent. Every action is controlled. Food, movement, speech, and even thought are regulated. This conditioning trains men and women to obey.

It makes them compliant not only inside prison but after release.

The threat of return hangs over them. Fear keeps them in line. The warehouse creates broken souls who are easier to govern.

The rituals of prison life reinforce the system. Head counts, roll calls, uniforms, and schedules all mimic military discipline. The prisoner becomes a cog in a machine. His individuality is erased. The system treats him as stock to be managed.

His humanity is ignored.

This is not rehabilitation. It is conditioning for servitude.

Examples show the cruelty. A man jailed for unpaid fines is warehoused until payment is made. A woman imprisoned for minor policy violations is held as if she were a danger to society.

Lives are destroyed not because harm was caused but because contracts were breached.

These cases prove that prisons are not about justice. They are about enforcing hidden contracts through confinement.

The language of sentencing confirms this. A man is "given time." Time becomes a commodity to be traded. He must "serve" years as if paying a debt. This reveals the commercial basis. Time is money.

A prison sentence is a financial instrument disguised as punishment.

The man pays not with coin but with his body and his years. The state profits from both.

Media presents prisons as necessary evils. Films and documentaries show hardened criminals behind bars. The message is that prisons protect society. The rare stories of violence and danger inside are magnified.

The daily reality of warehousing ordinary men and women for policy violations is hidden.

The illusion is maintained. The public is told to fear crime and to trust the warehouse system.

Education supports the myth. Children are told that prisons are for bad people. They are not told that prisons are businesses. They are not told that incarceration generates revenue. They are not told that many prisoners caused no harm to others.

The conditioning begins early.

By adulthood, most accept prisons as natural parts of society, never questioning their commercial roots.

Remedy begins with knowledge. The man who understands that prison is commerce sees the system clearly.

He knows that his body is treated as inventory. He knows that numbers and accounts drive the process.

This knowledge does not free him instantly, but it gives him strength.

It replaces fear with understanding. It allows him to stand in honour even when confined.

Stories of resistance exist. Some men and women have challenged imprisonment by questioning jurisdiction. They asked: Who is being held. Where is the contract. What obligation binds the living soul. In some cases, proceedings were halted. In others, sentences were shortened.

These stories are not widely known, but they show that the system fears exposure.

It thrives on ignorance. Knowledge is its enemy.

Practical steps follow. If faced with imprisonment, always remember that you are a living man or woman. Do not accept the label of inmate without protest. Demand proof of contract. Ask for evidence of consent. Refuse to be silent.

Even within the walls, honour can be maintained.

The system cannot extinguish truth. It can only confine bodies. Souls remain free.

The role of community is also vital. When men and women outside expose the truth of prisons, pressure builds. Campaigns, protests, and recordings reveal that prisons are warehouses. They show that incarceration is about revenue, not safety. Public awareness weakens the illusion.

It makes it harder for governments to justify endless confinement.

Truth spreads, and chains begin to loosen.

History offers examples of resistance to prisons.

Reformers in the past exposed debtor's jails and forced change. Movements revealed abuses in labour camps and forced closures. Each time the truth was spoken, the illusion weakened. Today the same courage is needed.

The warehouse system must be revealed for what it is: commerce, not justice.

Ask yourself direct questions. Did you ever consent to be warehoused? Did you ever sign a contract agreeing to be numbered and stored. Did you ever give permission to be traded as inventory. The answer is no. The system relies on silence.

It assumes consent where none was given.

That is the fraud at the heart of imprisonment.

Prisons are warehouses of the state. They are not centres of justice. They are places where bodies are stored for profit. They reduce men and women to numbers and contracts. They thrive on fear, ignorance, and compliance.

Once you see this, the walls lose their power.

They remain stone and steel, but they cannot confine the truth.

The deeper lesson is that freedom begins in the mind. Even behind bars, the living soul is free if it refuses the role of inmate. Knowledge and honour keep the spirit alive. The warehouse cannot crush truth.

It can only attempt to hide it.

The man or woman who knows this walks free even when confined.

The chapters ahead will explore banks and debt. Like prisons, they are warehouses: not for bodies but for wealth and promises. Together they form the cage of hidden contracts. Police feed the prisons. Prisons feed the banks. Banks feed the state.

It is one system.

To break free, you must see each link for what it is. The warehouse is only one part of the chain. Knowledge of it brings you closer to freedom.

Chapter 8: Banks: The Masters of Debt Illusion

Banks are presented as the heart of prosperity. They are described as engines of growth, pillars of stability, and trusted guardians of wealth. The logos, the marble buildings, and the polished suits all project power and security.

Yet the truth is far different.

Banks are not creators of wealth. They are masters of illusion. They create nothing but debt, and through debt they enslave nations, communities, and individuals. The living man or woman is trapped in a cycle of promises, contracts, and interest.

The Creation of Money

The greatest illusion of banking is money itself. Most people believe banks lend out deposits collected from savers. They believe that when a loan is granted, the money already exists. In reality, banks create money out of nothing.

When you sign a loan agreement, the bank types numbers into an account.

Those numbers did not exist before. They were created by your promise to repay. The so-called loan is nothing but a ledger entry, backed by your labour and your consent.

Central banks admit this openly. Reports from the Bank of England and the Federal Reserve state clearly that money is created when banks issue loans. Yet the public is never told. Schools still teach that banks lend from savings.

This lie keeps the illusion alive.

In truth, all modern money is debt. Every pound, dollar, or euro in circulation is owed to a bank, with interest attached.

Loans as Contracts of Servitude

When a man takes a loan, he believes he has borrowed money from a bank. What actually happens is that he has created credit for himself. The bank provides nothing but a signature on paper.

Yet the man is bound by contract to repay with interest.

The contract is enforced by courts, backed by police, and supported by prisons. A piece of paper creates a lifetime of servitude. The borrower never realises that he funded the transaction himself with his promise.

Mortgages show this clearly. Families believe the bank has lent them money to buy a house. In fact, the bank has typed numbers into an account based on the borrower's signature. The house is then held as collateral.

If payments are missed, the house is taken.

The bank loses nothing. It never risked anything real. The family loses years of labour and their home. This is the debt illusion at work.

Interest: The Endless Trap

Interest is the tool that makes the illusion profitable. For every loan, the bank demands repayment plus interest. Yet the money to pay interest is never created. Only the principal is created as debt.

This means that at all times there is less money in circulation than is owed.

The result is inevitable: defaults, foreclosures, and bankruptcies. The system requires failure.

It thrives on it. Every repossession strengthens the bank. Every bankruptcy transfers assets from the people to the system.

Credit cards are another trap. A man buys goods with a piece of plastic. The bank creates numbers out of nothing to pay the seller. The man then spends years paying back far more than he borrowed.

Late fees, penalties, and compounding interest keep him chained.

The goods are consumed quickly, but the debt lingers for decades. The card is marketed as freedom. In truth it is a collar.

The Illusion of Savings

Even savings accounts are part of the trick. A saver believes his money is held safely by the bank. In truth, the deposit becomes property of the bank. The saver is only an unsecured creditor.

If the bank fails, the saver joins the line of claimants.

The so-called guarantee schemes are limited, funded by taxpayers, and often worthless in crisis. The saver is not safe. He is a creditor lending money to a corporation that creates debt for profit.

The 2008 Crash: A Case Study

The crash of 2008 revealed the fraud. Banks created mountains of debt through mortgages, derivatives, and speculation. When the system collapsed, governments bailed them out with public money. The people lost homes, jobs, and savings, while banks received trillions.

Not a single major banker went to prison.

The lesson was clear: banks are too powerful to fail, but the people are never too small to be sacrificed.

The crash proved that banks are not guardians of stability. They are predators that feed on crisis. They profit when the bubble grows, and they profit again when it bursts. The cycle repeats because the illusion is never questioned.

The borrower still believes he owes real money.

The saver still believes the bank holds wealth. The truth is hidden in plain sight: all of it is debt, created from signatures and enforced by fear.

Digital Money and Total Control

The rise of digital currency strengthens the illusion. Cash once gave some freedom. A man could exchange notes privately without records. Today, banks push society toward a cashless world. Digital payments, online banking, and central bank digital currencies are sold as convenient.

In truth they are tools of surveillance and control.

Every transaction is tracked. Every purchase is recorded. Accounts can be frozen with a keystroke. The illusion of freedom fades as the chains of debt become digital.

Cryptocurrencies are presented as alternatives, but even they are drawn into regulation. Exchanges require identification. Transactions are monitored. Governments plan to integrate them into the system. The dream of escape is pulled back into the cage of commerce.

The masters of debt adapt, always seeking to preserve the illusion.

The Role of Courts and Police

Courts and police serve the banks. Every repossession, foreclosure, or debt collection relies on force. A family that refuses to leave a foreclosed home is dragged out by officers.

A man who defaults on payments is taken to court and treated as a criminal.

Judges enforce contracts without question. Police act as enforcers of commercial paper. The bank creates debt out of nothing, and the full power of the state ensures repayment. This is not justice. It is slavery by contract.

Symbols of Banking

The symbols of banks reveal their nature. Columns and marble mimic temples of old. Logos often include pyramids, eyes, and suns: marks of hidden power. The language of banking is full of ritual: bonds, notes, deposits, credits, debits.

Each term has roots in commerce and religion.

The bank is not a financial service. It is a temple of debt illusion. Clerks are priests. Account managers are confessors. Contracts are sacraments binding the soul.

Stories of Resistance

Some men and women have resisted the illusion. They challenged banks to produce proof of a loan. They asked: What substance was lent. Where was the risk. Many times banks could not answer. Cases collapsed when contracts were questioned with honour.

Others refused to act as the Strawman.

They separated themselves from the legal fiction and stood as living men.

Success stories are whispered, not broadcast. The system fears exposure. It survives on silence.

Practical Remedies

The first step is knowledge. See banks for what they are: creators of debt, not wealth. Understand that loans are contracts where you provide the value. Ask for proof of obligation. Demand evidence that real money was lent.

Insist on wet ink signatures.

Do not be afraid to question. Fear is the bank's greatest weapon.

Practical remedies include conditional acceptance. State that you will repay if the bank proves that value was lent. Demand the original note, not a copy. Many times the original is lost or destroyed. Without it, no lawful claim exists.

Stand in honour, but stand firm.

Knowledge of maxims gives strength: he who asserts must prove, consent makes law, no one is obliged to accept a benefit.

Community remedies are also vital. Men and women supporting each other against repossession have saved homes. Groups that record and expose foreclosures weaken the illusion. Public awareness grows when the fraud is seen. The bank fears exposure.

It thrives in secrecy but falters in light.

The Psychology of Debt

Debt is more than numbers. It is psychological control. A man in debt feels shame. He works harder, fears loss, and obeys more easily. A family burdened by mortgages or credit cards sacrifices freedom for security.

They avoid risk, avoid protest, and avoid challenge.

Debt becomes a leash around the soul. Banks know this. They use debt not only for profit but for control.

Advertising reinforces this. Banks present loans as dreams fulfilled. Holidays, cars, homes, and gadgets are dangled as rewards. Credit is painted as freedom. In truth it is slavery dressed in luxury. The goods fade but the debt remains.

The man forgets the pleasure but feels the chain.

This psychological trap is more powerful than bars of steel.

Nations in Debt

The illusion extends to nations. Governments borrow from central banks, creating debt for entire populations. Interest payments consume tax revenues. Services are cut while banks grow rich. The people are told they must tighten belts, accept austerity, and pay more tax.

All of it serves to feed the debt machine.

Nations are warehouses of debt just as prisons are warehouses of bodies. Citizens become collateral for government loans.

Breaking the Illusion

The remedy is simple but difficult. Refuse the illusion. See that banks create nothing. Understand that value comes from you, not from them. Stop fearing debt collectors. Ask for contracts, not threats. Stand as the living man, not the Strawman.

Refuse to be tricked into servitude.

The illusion breaks when it is seen. Banks have no power without belief.

Ask yourself direct questions. Did the bank lend you anything of substance. Did it risk its own wealth.

Did you consent knowingly to a lifetime of servitude. The answer is no. You were deceived. You were bound by illusion.

The power of banks rests on your ignorance.

Knowledge is freedom. Honour is strength. Courage is the key.

Closing.

Banks are the masters of debt illusion. They create nothing, yet they own everything. They build palaces from promises and enslave nations with numbers. They are not guardians of wealth but harvesters of labour. They thrive on silence, fear, and ignorance.

Once you see the trick, the spell is broken.

The man who knows the truth is no longer a debtor but a sovereign. The woman who refuses consent is no longer collateral but free.

The next chapters will continue to reveal the chains. Courts, prisons, and banks are one system. Each depends on the other. Debt feeds prisons, prisons feed banks, banks feed the state. Together they form the cage of hidden contracts.

Knowledge of this cage is the first step toward freedom.

The masters of illusion fear nothing more than exposure. Speak the truth, and the illusion crumbles.

Chapter 9: Education, The Programming of Obedience

Education is presented as the key to opportunity. It is described as the path to knowledge, prosperity, and freedom.

Schools are portrayed as places where young minds are opened, where critical thinking is encouraged, and where the next generation is prepared to lead.

Yet the reality is far different. Education in the modern age is not about liberation but about programming. It is designed to produce obedient workers, compliant citizens, and passive consumers. From the first day of school to the last day of schooling.

The Origins of Compulsory Schooling

Compulsory schooling arose not to empower but to control. In the nineteenth century, governments in Europe and America made education mandatory. The stated purpose was literacy and citizenship. The hidden purpose was obedience.

Industrial society needed workers who could follow orders, read instructions, and show up on time.

Schools were designed to train children to fit into factories and offices. Bells mimicked factory whistles. Desks in rows mirrored assembly lines. The teacher acted as a foreman.

The system succeeded. Generations grew up believing that success meant conformity. Those who obeyed earned certificates and jobs.

Those who resisted were labelled failures. The lesson was not knowledge but submission.

School became the first training ground for life inside the cage of hidden contracts.

The Curriculum of Control

Modern curricula reinforce the same pattern. Children are taught facts and figures but rarely taught how to think. Memorisation replaces inquiry. Testing replaces creativity. Obedience is rewarded more than curiosity. Subjects like history are presented through the lens of state power.

Wars, treaties, and rulers are emphasised, while stories of resistance are hidden.

Economics is taught as if debt and banking were natural, not as illusions. Law is taught as statute, not as consent.

Critical questions are discouraged. A student who asks why taxes are compulsory or why banks create money from nothing is quickly silenced. Teachers are bound by guidelines that prevent them from straying beyond official narratives.

The message is clear: do not question, repeat.

Education becomes indoctrination.

Symbols and Rituals of Obedience

The structure of schools is filled with rituals that teach submission. Uniforms erase individuality. Bells dictate movement. Permission must be asked to speak, move, or even use the toilet. Examinations rank and sort children, creating competition rather than cooperation.

Authority is always external: the teacher, the principal, the inspector.

The child learns that freedom is granted by others, not natural.

This conditioning prepares him to obey employers, officials, and officers later in life.

Assemblies, pledges, and ceremonies reinforce the message. Children stand in lines, recite oaths, and salute flags. They are trained to honour symbols rather than truth. These rituals seem harmless but shape deep habits of obedience.

By the time adulthood arrives, compliance is second nature.

The Weight of Testing

Standardised testing has become the idol of modern education. Governments demand results. Schools focus on exams above all else. Children learn to fear failure, to associate worth with scores, and to equate obedience with success. Creativity is crushed. Individual strengths are ignored.

The child becomes a number, a statistic, a result in a league table.

Testing serves the system, not the child. It sorts future workers into categories. It identifies those suited to technical roles, bureaucratic roles, or menial labour. It does not nurture free thinkers. It weeds them out.

The illusion of merit hides the reality of programming.

Universities and the Debt Trap

For those who succeed in school, the next step is university. Universities are portrayed as temples of knowledge and freedom of thought. In truth they are extensions of the same system. Degrees are marketed as tickets to success.

Students are told they must borrow to invest in their future.

Student loans are the modern form of bondage.

Young men and women sign contracts at eighteen that bind them for decades.

They believe they are borrowing money from the government or banks.

In reality they are creating debt instruments secured by their future labour.

Universities raise fees knowing that easy credit will cover the cost. Banks and governments profit. Students graduate with certificates and chains.

The weight of debt shapes choices. Graduates avoid risk, avoid questioning, and accept jobs they dislike to make payments. They postpone families, homes, and freedom. Debt becomes a leash around their lives. Education, sold as liberation, becomes servitude.

The Corporate Influence

Corporations shape education at every level. Textbooks are written to suit official narratives. Sponsorships brand schools with corporate logos. Universities tailor courses to corporate needs. The goal is not free inquiry but workforce preparation.

Students are trained to serve industries, not to challenge them.

Media and technology reinforce the same programming. Educational television, online platforms, and even children's apps present official versions of history, science, and economics. Rarely is dissent allowed.

The child grows up in an environment where every source of knowledge repeats the same message: obey, consume, comply.

Discipline and Surveillance

Modern schools use surveillance as part of training. Cameras monitor corridors.

Attendance is tracked electronically. Behaviour is logged and stored. Even expressions and attitudes are recorded in some systems.

This teaches children that they are always watched, that privacy does not exist, and that authority has the right to monitor every action.

This prepares them for adult life in a surveillance society.

Discipline reinforces the lesson. Detentions, suspensions, and expulsions punish those who resist. Rarely is harm to others the reason. More often the punishment is for defiance, questioning, or non-compliance. The system does not tolerate free thinkers.

It labels them troublemakers, isolates them, and pushes them out.

Obedience is the only acceptable path.

Stories of Resistance

Despite the system, stories of resistance exist. Some students have challenged the curriculum, demanding to know why certain truths are hidden. Others have refused to wear uniforms, seeing them as symbols of control.

Some parents have withdrawn children from schools, choosing homeschooling or community learning.

In many cases, these children thrive. They develop creativity, independence, and courage. Their stories are not publicised because they expose the weakness of the system.

Practical Remedies

Remedy begins with awareness. Parents and students must see schools as programming, not liberation.

This does not mean rejecting knowledge but rejecting indoctrination. Knowledge is power when sought freely, not when imposed as control.

Homeschooling is one path. Families who take responsibility for education can tailor learning to honour, creativity, and truth. Community schooling is another. Groups of families can teach each other, share resources, and create environments of freedom. Self-education is also vital.

Books, online resources, and independent inquiry allow men and women to grow without chains.

The key is to remember that education is a choice. The system sells it as compulsory. But knowledge belongs to the free. Consent is required. No one can be forced to learn lies unless he accepts them.

The living man or woman who stands in truth can reject indoctrination and seek wisdom instead.

The Psychological Cage

Education not only conditions behaviour but shapes identity. A child who is told for years that success equals obedience internalises the lesson. He begins to see himself not as a free being but as a role: student, worker, citizen.

His self-worth is tied to external approval.

This is the psychological cage. Even after leaving school, he continues to seek grades in the form of promotions, performance reviews, and pay rises. He lives for approval, not for truth.

Advertising exploits this. Corporations market products to students as symbols of identity. Phones, clothes, and technology become status markers. The child learns that value comes from consumption, not from inner worth.

Education and advertising combine to produce the perfect consumer: obedient, insecure, and dependent.

Universities as Gatekeepers

Universities guard the gates of the system. Degrees are required for many professions. Without them, opportunities vanish. This gives universities immense power. They can dictate content, raise fees, and shape society. Yet most degrees have little to do with knowledge.

They are signals of obedience: proof that a man or woman sat through years of programming without rebellion.

Employers see the degree not as wisdom but as compliance.

The result is generations saddled with debt, programmed for obedience, and convinced they are free. The illusion is complete. Education has done its work.

Breaking the Illusion

The remedy is to see education as it is. Knowledge is not owned by schools, universities, or corporations. It belongs to the free. The internet, libraries, and communities contain more wisdom than any official curriculum.

The man who seeks truth independently is more educated than the graduate burdened by debt and indoctrination.

Parents must reclaim responsibility. Do not hand children to the state without question. Question the curriculum. Teach honour, creativity, and freedom at home. Encourage curiosity rather than obedience. Support communities of learning that reject debt and indoctrination.

Students must also awaken. Do not equate grades with worth. Do not believe that debt is the price of knowledge. Question everything. Stand in truth even when teachers frown. The system cannot bind the living soul who refuses to consent.

Closing.

Education is the programming of obedience. It is sold as freedom but delivers servitude. Schools condition children to obey. Universities chain them with debt. Corporations shape curricula to create workers and consumers. The illusion is powerful but fragile.

Once you see it, the spell is broken.

Ask yourself: Did you ever consent to be programmed. Did you ever sign a contract agreeing to debt before you understood it. Did you ever agree to surrender your creativity for grades. The answer is no. Consent was assumed.

The fraud was hidden.

The living man or woman is not a student, not a debtor, not a worker. He is free. She is sovereign. Knowledge belongs to them, not to the state. Education can be reclaimed.

It can become a path to truth once more, but only when obedience is rejected.

The programming must be undone. Honour must replace fear. Curiosity must replace conformity.

The cage of education is only one part of the system of hidden contracts. Banks, prisons, and police all depend on it. The child must be programmed to obey before the other chains can be attached.

Once the programming fails, the entire system begins to collapse.

That is why education is so central. That is why breaking free is so urgent.

Chapter 10: The Media, Masters of Perception

Media is presented as the voice of truth. Newspapers claim to inform. Television anchors present themselves as neutral guides. Online platforms boast of connecting people and empowering voices. The logos, jingles, and polished presenters all project authority.

Yet the deeper reality is very different.

Media is not a tool of truth but a weapon of perception. It exists to shape thought, control opinion, and reinforce obedience. It tells the people what to fear, what to desire, and what to ignore.

The Roots of Media Power

From the earliest days of the printing press, rulers saw the power of controlling information. Monarchs and governments granted licences only to friendly publishers. Dissenting voices were silenced. With the rise of radio and television, the control deepened.

Broadcast required government permission, so only approved voices could speak.

The illusion of free press was created, but in reality every outlet was tied to state or corporate interests.

Today, a handful of corporations control most global media. Newspapers, television stations, film studios, and digital platforms are owned by conglomerates with deep ties to banks and governments. The supposed diversity of opinion is an illusion. Different logos, same owners.

Different anchors, same script.

This concentration ensures that narratives are consistent and that dissent is marginalised.

News as Programming

News is presented as neutral reporting. In truth it is programming. Stories are selected, framed, and repeated to create perception. Fear is the primary tool. Crime, war, disease, and disaster dominate headlines.

The message is constant: the world is dangerous, and only authority can keep you safe.

This fear weakens critical thought and makes the public more compliant.

Repetition reinforces the programming. A phrase is repeated across outlets until it becomes accepted truth. During wars, identical wording appears in dozens of newspapers. During financial crises, talking points are echoed across television and radio.

The technique is simple: say it often enough, and belief follows.

Symbols of Authority

Media uses symbols to command trust. Anchors sit at desks in suits, surrounded by screens and maps. Logos feature globes, eagles, or eyes: symbols of global power. Music and graphics create drama. These cues tell the subconscious that authority is speaking.

The viewer relaxes and accepts.

The ritual is as formal as any courtroom or church service. The goal is not information but belief.

Case Study: War Reporting

War reporting shows media's role clearly. Governments frame conflicts as battles of good against evil. Media repeats the script.

Enemy leaders are demonised, allies are glorified, and civilian deaths are minimised. Reporters are embedded with armies, ensuring they see only one side.

Lies become accepted history.

Weapons of mass destruction, humanitarian interventions, liberation campaigns: all repeated until the public consents to war.

When the truth emerges years later, the damage is done. The war has been fought, the contracts signed, the resources seized. Media never apologises. It moves on to the next narrative. Perception has been managed, obedience secured.

Case Study: Financial Crises

During financial crises, media plays the same role. In 2008, the public was told that banks were too big to fail, that bailouts were necessary, and that taxpayers must foot the bill.

Little attention was paid to the fraud of money creation, the greed of bankers, or the destruction of families.

The narrative was that sacrifice was patriotic and inevitable. The public accepted austerity, while bankers celebrated bonuses.

Again, the message was clear: trust authority, obey policy, pay the price. Media did not inform. It programmed compliance.

Case Study: Health and Fear

Health crises provide another example. Outbreaks are reported with apocalyptic tones. Charts, graphics, and death counts dominate screens. Fear grips the population.

Demands for obedience follow: accept restrictions, trust experts, surrender freedoms. Alternative voices are silenced as dangerous.

Media frames dissent as conspiracy.

The result is mass compliance, even when policies destroy livelihoods and communities. The narrative is maintained until obedience is secured.

The Rise of Digital Media

In the modern era, digital platforms have become as powerful as newspapers and television once were. Social media presents itself as open and democratic. Anyone can speak, anyone can share. In truth, algorithms decide what is seen and what is hidden.

Platforms promote certain voices and suppress others.

Entire narratives can be amplified or buried by unseen code.

This algorithmic control is more powerful than censorship. The user believes he is choosing what to see, but the platform chooses for him. Posts that support official narratives are boosted. Posts that question authority are shadow-banned or deleted.

Influencers are rewarded for obedience and punished for dissent.

The system trains millions without them realising.

The Attention Economy

Digital media thrives on attention. Outrage, fear, and desire generate clicks. Platforms design feeds to keep users hooked. Endless scrolling, notifications, and personalised content exploit psychology. The result is addiction.

People spend hours consuming curated narratives. Critical thought fades.

Perception is managed by distraction.

Important issues vanish under floods of gossip, celebrity drama, and trivial outrage.

This is not accidental. It is programming. The distracted mind cannot resist. The fearful mind cannot question. Media, old and new, serves the same master: obedience through perception.

Social Media as Surveillance

Beyond distraction, social media is a tool of surveillance. Every like, share, and comment is recorded. Profiles are built. Behaviour is predicted. Governments and corporations use this data to target messages, manipulate opinions, and anticipate resistance.

The illusion of freedom hides total monitoring.

The user is both consumer and product.

Whistle-blowers have revealed how platforms cooperate with states to shape opinion. Content is flagged, accounts suspended, and narratives controlled. This is not free speech. It is managed speech. The perception of freedom is maintained while the reality of control deepens.

Stories of Resistance

Despite this, independent voices break through. Alternative media outlets, bloggers, and citizen journalists expose lies.

Recordings of wars, protests, and police abuses bypass mainstream filters. Communities share truth across networks. These stories show the cracks in the system.

The illusion is strong but not invincible.

Truth spreads when men and women refuse to be silent.

Examples abound. Independent researchers exposed false claims about wars. Bloggers revealed corruption hidden by official media. Citizens filmed abuses that would otherwise have been denied. These acts prove that perception can be reclaimed when truth is spoken.

Practical Remedies

The first step is discernment. Do not accept stories at face value. Ask who benefits. Ask who owns the outlet. Ask why the story is told now. These questions reveal bias.

The second step is diversity. Do not rely on one source. Seek independent voices. Compare narratives. The truth lies not in a single outlet but in the patterns across many.

The third step is refusal to consent. Do not allow fear to dictate obedience. When media demands submission, pause. Ask if harm is real or manufactured. Refuse to be driven by panic. Fear is their weapon. Calm is your defence.

The Psychology of Media

Media shapes not only opinions but emotions. It tells you when to fear, when to hope, when to celebrate, and when to mourn. It conditions collective moods.

The public laughs at the same jokes, cries at the same tragedies, and rages at the same enemies.

This shared perception creates unity, but it is false unity under authority. The individual is swept into the crowd, his will dissolved.

Advertising deepens this control. Commercials associate products with emotions.

Happiness, success, and love are tied to brands. The consumer buys not goods but identities. Media trains people to define themselves by consumption.

The obedient worker, shaped by schools and bound by debt, becomes the obedient consumer, shaped by screens and bound by desire.

Breaking the Spell

The remedy is to break the spell. Limit exposure. Disconnect from endless feeds. Seek truth deliberately rather than passively. Question authority, even when dressed in suits and logos. Teach children that media is manipulation, not truth.

Build communities that value firsthand experience over secondhand narratives.

The living man or woman must reclaim perception. Truth is not given by anchors or algorithms. It is found by honour, courage, and inquiry. Consent to media is not required. You choose what to believe. You choose what to accept.

Closing.

Media is the master of perception. It shapes thought, controls emotion, and directs obedience. Newspapers, television, and digital platforms all serve the same purpose: to maintain the system of hidden contracts. They thrive on fear, distraction, and repetition.

They are temples of illusion, not fountains of truth.

Ask yourself: Did you ever consent to be programmed. Did you ever sign a contract agreeing to be manipulated by news and screens. Did you ever agree to surrender your perception to corporations. The answer is no. Consent was assumed.

The fraud was hidden.

The living man or woman who sees through the illusion is free. Perception belongs to the sovereign, not to the system. Truth is not a broadcast but a choice. Honour breaks the spell. Courage protects perception.

Once media loses its power, the cage begins to crack.

The masters of illusion fear nothing more than the awakening of the people.

Chapter 11: The Path to Freedom

Standing in Honour

The first step on the path to freedom is to stand in honour. Honour is the foundation of remedy. It means you do not lie, you do not cheat, and you do not cause harm. The system is designed to pull you into dishonour, to make you angry, or to provoke you into argument.

When you fall into that trap, you provide them with the excuse they need to treat you as a subject of their rules.

Standing in honour is simple: remain calm, remain truthful, and remain firm. If an officer demands your name, ask who is making the claim. If a letter demands payment, request the signed agreement that proves obligation. If a judge asks for a plea, ask who is the injured party.

By standing in honour, you shift the burden of proof back to the claimant. Without proof, there is no case.

Using Notice and Record

The most powerful tool in your hands is the written notice. A notice is a declaration of truth and position. It is evidence on the record. The state survives on presumption. It thrives on silence. When you remain silent, it assumes consent. When you reply with clear notices, it is forced to confront your position.

Conditional acceptance is one of the strongest forms of notice. It is not refusal, it is not confrontation. It is acceptance upon conditions that must be met.

For example: 'I will pay upon proof of obligation, proof of contract, and proof of authority.' This is honourable, simple, and impossible for most officials to satisfy.

They have no proof, only presumption.

Keep your notices simple. Use plain words. Always keep copies. Send by recorded delivery when possible. If you are taken to court, your notices become your evidence of honour. They show that you did not refuse, you did not ignore, and you did not consent to fraud.

Withdrawing Consent

Every hidden contract relies on consent. Sometimes that consent is explicit, such as when you sign an application. More often, it is implied. Each time you answer to the NAME in capital letters, each time you use a licence, each time you comply with a notice without question, you provide implied consent.

The path to freedom is learning how to withdraw that consent.

Withdrawing consent does not mean living in conflict. It means making clear that you do not accept obligations without evidence.

You can say: 'I do not consent to any contract unless all terms are disclosed and agreed.' You can write: 'I reserve all rights and waive none.' These words may seem small, but they shift the balance of power. They remind officials that consent is required, and that you are aware of your rights.

Building Community

Freedom is not a solitary journey. The system thrives on isolation.

It counts on each man and woman standing alone, afraid of authority and unaware of remedy. When communities stand together, the fraud weakens. Knowledge shared is power multiplied.

Communities can meet weekly to study remedy. They can share templates for notices. They can attend court hearings to witness and support each other. If one man is harassed by a bank, others can flood the bank with lawful notices.

If one woman is summoned by a council, others can accompany her and hold the officials to account. The power of community is immense, and it is feared by those who rely on division.

Living the Remedy

Freedom is more than paperwork. It is a way of life. Remedy must be lived daily. It is not only for the courtroom or the council office. It is for the family, the workplace, and the community. Living remedy means practising truth in speech, fairness in trade, and responsibility in actions.

Practical steps are simple: refuse to answer as the Strawman. Keep your own records. Question every demand that comes without proof. Always ask: 'Who makes the claim? What evidence do you have?' Over time, these habits become natural. They shift your posture from subject to sovereign.

Overcoming Fear

The greatest weapon of the system is fear. Letters are written to intimidate. Courts are designed to overawe. Uniforms are meant to scare. Fear paralyses men and women and forces them into consent. To overcome fear, you must remember a simple truth: they rely on your agreement.

Without it, their power is paper.

Fear fades with knowledge. The more you practise notices, the more you study law, the more you attend hearings as an observer, the less intimidating the process becomes. Fear thrives in darkness. Shine the light of truth on it, and it shrinks. Stand calmly. Breathe. Speak simply. Ask for evidence. Fear cannot survive in honour.

Teaching the Next Generation

The path to freedom is not only for today. It is for tomorrow. Children are born free, but they are quickly registered, numbered, and conditioned. To break this cycle, knowledge must pass from one generation to the next.

Teach children the difference between the living being and the Strawman. Teach them that consent is theirs to give or withhold. Teach them that law is not the same as legislation, and that honour is the highest rule. When the next generation grows up aware, the hidden contracts will no longer trap them.

The Door Is Open

This book has revealed the hidden contracts. It has shown how governments, banks, and courts rely on presumption and consent. It has shown that freedom is not granted by the state but is lived by the man or woman who claims it. The door to freedom is open.

To step through, you need no permission, no licence, no application. You need only to stand in honour, to use notices, to withdraw consent from fraud, and to live in truth.

The path is not easy, but it is simple. Each step you take weakens the fraud. Each act of honour strengthens your freedom.

The chains are paper. The key is consent. The choice is yours. Walk in truth, and no man or institution can enslave you.

Final Notes

This book is a beginning, not an end. The habits that bind most people, answering to the NAME, obeying unproven paper, pleading to policies, were built over years. They unwind through steady practice.

Keep your language short, your questions clear, and your records tidy.

Do not argue. Require proof. Do not rage. Remain in honour. Your posture teaches others more than your words.

Share templates freely, but remember that remedy is a posture, not a script. If you must speak ten words, make nine of them questions.

When officials meet a calm man or woman standing on truth, many step back to policy and leave you to peace.

if you stumble, begin again. Freedom is a muscle. It strengthens with use.

May these pages help you see offers where others see orders, neighbours where others see numbers, and light where others see walls. Walk well. Keep your word. And always remember: consent is yours to give, or withhold.

Don't miss out!

Visit the website below and you can sign up to receive emails whenever Roger Davies publishes a new book. There's no charge and no obligation.

https://books2read.com/r/B-A-HHGNE-PKLXG

BOOKS 2 READ

Connecting independent readers to independent writers.

Did you love *The Hidden Contracts: How Governments Enslave the People*? Then you should read *The Sovereign Path: Living Free Beyond the System*[1] by Roger Davies!

[2]

Most people who wake up to the system stop at awareness. They see the hidden contracts, the legal fictions, the taxes, the courts, and the tricks of authority. They know something is wrong but remain trapped in daily life. They ask the same question: what do I do now.

The Sovereign Path is the answer. This final book in the series moves beyond exposing fraud and presumption. It shows how to live free every day as a man or woman in honour. It is not a book of theory but a practical guide to standing outside the cage.

Roger Davies walks you through the essential steps of living sovereignty in practice:

1. https://books2read.com/u/3yw9OZ

2. https://books2read.com/u/3yw9OZ

• Standing as a living man or woman and refusing to be treated as a legal fiction• Guarding your consent so it is never given by silence, fear, or mistake• Using conditional acceptance to shift the burden of proof back to claimants• Writing affidavits and notices that place truth on the record and remove presumption• Creating private agreements that honour standing without inviting state control• Trading, bartering, and exchanging value outside the debt system• Raising children in truth, building family strength, and passing freedom forward• Growing food, creating shelter, and securing the basics of life without endless licences• Finding fellowship with other men and women on the same path• Overcoming fear, ridicule, and the pressure to submit

This book is about action, not argument. It shows that the cage was never locked. The only bars are ignorance, fear, and habit. Once you see that, you are free to walk through the gate.

The Sovereign Path explains why honour is the shield that cannot be pierced, why consent is the key to every hidden contract, and why silence is treated as agreement. It shows how a simple pause before signing or answering can change everything. It gives examples of real men and women who have used conditional acceptance and honourable notices to end claims, withdraw from contracts, and stand free.

But this book is not about isolation. Sovereignty is not retreat. It is community on equal terms. You will learn how to form private agreements, trade without permission, and build fellowship with others who choose the same path. The goal is not to fight the system but to make it irrelevant in your life.

The Sovereign Path is written for those who are ready to step from knowledge into action. It does not promise quick fixes or magic words. It offers principles, tools, and encouragement so that each reader can live sovereignty with integrity.

If you are tired of asking what to do next, if you are ready to live free in peace and honour, this book will show you the way forward. Freedom is already yours. The only step left is to live it.

Also by Roger Davies

Sovereign Foundations: Liberty, Rights, Consent

The Constitution of One: How the Bill of Rights Protects the Sovereign Man & Woman

From Subjects to Sovereigns: Reclaiming the Spirit of 1776

Liberty by Consent: Reclaiming Freedom Through the Law of Consent

Standalone

The Commonwealth Corporation: How Australia Was Turned Into a Business

The Legal Fiction: The Greatest Trick Ever Played on Humanity

The Sovereign Path: Living Free Beyond the System

Common Law: The True Law of the Living

Freedom by Rebuttal: How to Say No and Stand Free

The Magna Carta: Why It Is Important to Sovereign Men and Women

The Trust Game: Hidden Estates and the Cestui Que Vie Act

Freedom by Notice: Winning with Paperwork

The Hidden Contracts: How Governments Enslave the People

The Law of the Living: Admiralty Shadows and the Path to Sovereignty

About the Author

Roger Davies researches the crossroads of commerce, policy, and personal sovereignty. He writes for readers who sense there is more to the story, who are ready to replace fear with honour and paperwork with plain truth. When not writing, he helps men and women organise their records, challenge unfounded claims, and build communities grounded in mutual aid and responsibility.

www.ingramcontent.com/pod-product-compliance
Lightning Source LLC
LaVergne TN
LVHW022310200926
848481LV00004B/1263